Essays of a Convict

An American Third-Class Citizen

Written by:
Celestino "Sal" Colon

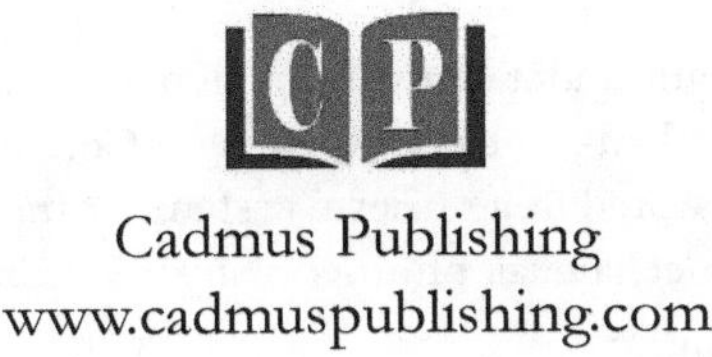

Cadmus Publishing
www.cadmuspublishing.com

Copyright © 2021 Celestino Colon

Cover art by Mr. Romano Ferraro

Published by Cadmus Publishing
www.cadmuspublishing.com
Port Angeles, WA

ISBN: 978-1-63751-086-5
Library of Congress Control Number: 2021923585

All rights reserved. Copyright under Berne Copyright Convention, Universal
Copyright Convention, and Pan-American Copyright Convention. No part of this
book may be reproduced, stored in a retrieval system, or transmitted in any form, or
by any means, electronic, mechanical, photocopying, recording or otherwise, without
prior permission of the author.

DEDICATION

This book is dedicated to my warm, loving and supportive parents. Examples of unconditional love: My Dad Celestino ("Big Sal") and Mom Edna.

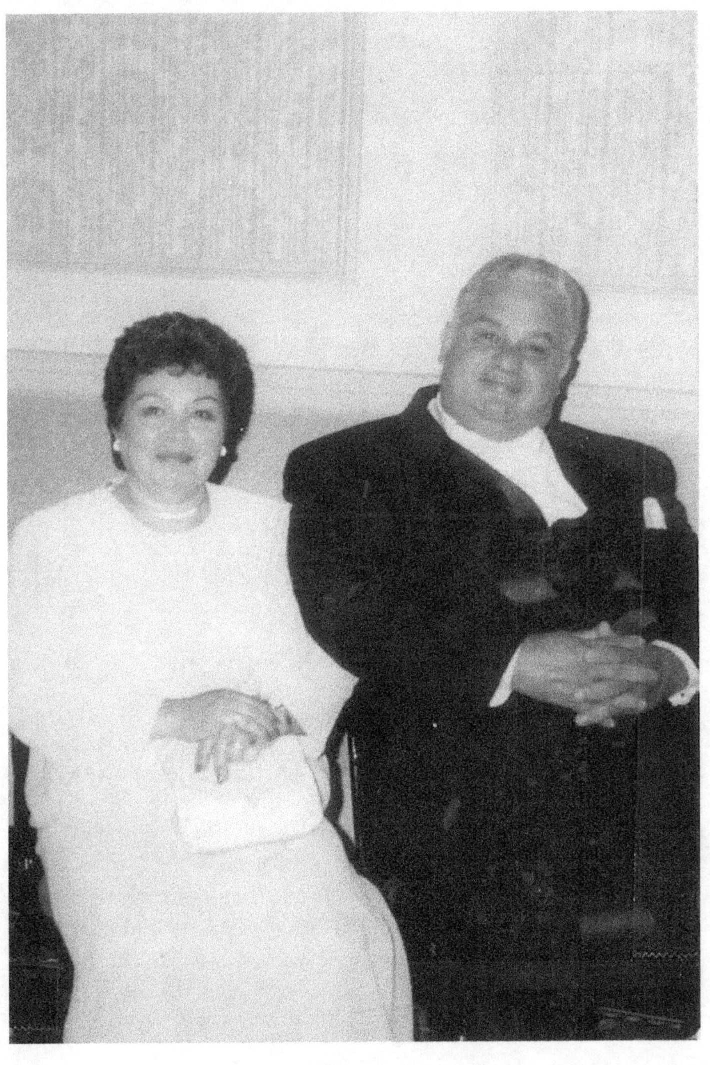

Preface (by Proxy)

Prison in America is an opaque structure, shielded from the eyes and ears of society through both separation and secrecy. Unless one works in a prison, or by the grace of God bravely ventures in as a volunteer, the operational and rehabilitative realities within correction go unseen due to a self-perpetuated correctional bureaucracy, a sensation-driven media and a lethargic, uninvolved populace.

In the first, there is neither a mechanism for holding prison staff accountable for unjust actions, nor a goal of rehabilitation against which their work can be measured as acceptable. In the second, stories of reformed prisoners displaying changed lives, whether inside prison or outside as reconciled citizens, are not deemed newsworthy, even though examples are legion. In the third, we have become comfortable in American society with an "out-of-sight, out-of-mind" mentality regarding criminals. "Lock 'em up, and throw away the key!" We cover our eyes and ears and believe that everything will be okay.

Thankfully, Freedom of Speech still exists in America, and prisoners are acknowledged as still retaining a right which, as a last resort, serves to shed light on the visceral activity within the belly of the beast. Because of the crypto-nature of today's carceral system, it is a book like this that reminds and reintroduces us to the humanity of a prisoner. When one comes in contact with the passion, love and humanity of a soul, ignorance can no longer be pleaded because that warehouse number has become a living, breathing, feeling and relatable intellect.

Sal's passion for justice and equity in prison is not a hypocritical ideal where what is good for authorities is not good for inmates, but is instead a consistent recognition that crime is wrong for prisoner and prison staff alike. His love for parents, fiancée and fellow inmates reveals a loyalty and brotherhood that should strike a virtuous chord in our hearts. His confession and repentance of sins and crimes, and his willingness to vulnerably air his dirty laundry publicly, should convict us all of the high bar that many of our own fearful hearts fail to meet.

Prison is a missionary field like no other. One cannot apply for a visa or citizenship to get into such a place. So, God must raise up missionaries from within, molding the worst of society into holy, selfless and sacrificial purveyors of truth and unconditional love. Sal's story is one where God took an angry, bitter man bent on retribution and troublemaking, and changed him into a Christlike soldier for justice. Administrators, captains, and assorted staff do not know what to make of Sal's miraculous transformation. True missionaries do not flee persecution but boldly go into the lions' den out of love for those to whom they are ministering.

Sal has been offered a deal: he can leave prison and move to England in exchange for dropping all lawsuits and forfeiting his right to litigate. His love for prisoners and intense desire to see prison reform come to fruition prevents him from leaving the battlefield. Someone once said to Jesus, "All these things will I give you, if you will fall down and worship me," to which Jesus replied in part, "You shall worship the Lord your God, and Him only shall you serve."

Beyond this preface lies a treasure you have never heard about, in a place you would not think to look for it. May it change the way you see and hear.

Jacques D. Robidoux

Old Colony

August 3rd, in the year of our Lord 2021

INTRODUCTION

I live in a prison. I have been incarcerated for decades. For too many years have I witnessed the destruction of lives and the decay of dreams.

Prison life is like none other. In prison, words are chosen carefully and are received with scrutiny, with a fight or even death just a comment away. We prisoners, in general, struggle unsuccessfully each day to cast off the shackles of our past. We speak in a tone of voice that is the essence of loneliness, a voice that only the lost and/or the abandoned can utter. We live a life devoid of hope and purpose.

I have come to realize that tears sometimes are the best words the heart can speak, but this world that I am living in does not allow for such language. You see, we all have a tendency to allow the past to supersede the present, especially in prison. I find that most prisoners are operating with impunity when they fight one another, but if the truth be told, prisoners in general lack the commitment to fight when it comes to their rights.

People in general need someone to whom they can divulge their sins and foibles, their weaknesses and heartaches. This is especially true of those incarcerated. Yet, most people in the free world are conditioned not to be disposed to cultivate prisoners' acquaintances. Human ears have heard, human eyes have seen and human hands have touched the world of life, but it seems many avoid prisoner contact at all costs. We are the world's social outcasts, the pariahs of society.

This is why I write. I believe that the more people read about prison life, the more informed and better equipped they will be to understand the importance of mending broken lives.

Some of the most poignant moments I have spent as a "Jailhouse lawyer" are those spent with other prisoners as they tell me about the road they took that landed them in prison. Some try all kinds of coping mechanisms in an attempt to survive this cruel world.

While many sit waiting for justice, with its flaws and ambiguities to prevail, I have chosen to voice my opinions and give a voice to all the injustices I see. I have minced no words in voicing my low opinion of the prison industry and its Mass Incarceration. In fact, I find it therapeutic. It has allowed me to break the monotony of prison life, though it has made me a persona non grata within the Massachusetts prison system.

Due to my writings, my litigation history and a profound penchant for civil disobedience, I have attained a de facto coup. Yet on a spiritual level, I get caught up between the proverbial rock and a hard place. My faith has given me courage in my convictions, strength in times of trouble and an unspeakable love for my fellow incarcerated brothers and sisters.

Of course, I have considered my own freedom, but only in the abstract. Fighting for those who cannot fight for their rights is my main concern. I have found a way to extricate myself from this situation, this world where the pain and loneliness prevail so profoundly.

For me personally, I have identified the origin of my tears and heartache. I have seen the truth of it all, with no easy euphemisms – after all, these past few years have only reminded me that my soul was still shackled to a ball of guilt that had been weighing me down. I do understand, and I have come to unequivocally identify the fact that the universe has a sense of irony. Sometimes you get reminded, too rudely at times, just how sadistic that can be.

I am a man of conviction, with a strong Christian faith, and my view of justice is simple and direct. I believe every man, woman and child should always strive for justice and peace. I am of the opinion that we have a moral obligation to humanity.

It has been said that a person's greatest virtue is the courage of one against all. I have bought into this philosophy. In a world of takers, I am a thinker and doer. My adversaries have found a way to amputate my rights by creating smoke screens in every facet of prison life. They have demonstrated to me by their collective actions that they are not one iota better than any prisoner I have ever met. They use a litany of devices to keep me down: lies, threats, coercion and physical and mental harms. (See "NCCI At Gardner: An Oxymoron's Haven.")

Therefore, knowing all of this, I have no qualms in sacrificing myself in the war I have felt so profoundly and passionately for: My heart's indignant cry for justice. I will not compromise my principles, even trading all potential chances for freedom in my attempt to bring justice into this dark and lonely world that I find myself in. This book of articles I have written is an outcry to others.

So yes, I write editorials, exposés and short stories of hope that depict the plight of prisoners (see "A Call to Humanity"). I want to enlighten people about our world (see "A Day of Reflection"). But, I also want to convey the importance of standing up and being counted (see "What Does It All Mean?").

I also need to convey to those that feel as though they are searching for some reason to make a difference, to make this world a better place, whether by acts of atonement or kindness, that they can do something (see "Changing the World From a

Prison Cell"). We all can make a difference.

Furthermore, I also need to speak from the heart (see "A Letter to Michelle") and even ask for forgiveness (see "Finally, Gina").

In conclusion, let us keep in mind that just because we have been dealt a certain hand in life, it does not mean that we can't choose to rise above it to try to retain whatever essential humanity we can gather. Enjoy "Essays from a Convict."

Celestino Colon

Contents

A Day of Reflection 1

A Eulogy from a Son (and Friend)...5

'To Love a Woman' 8

Changing the World from a Prison Cell 10

Circle of Caring.. 15

A Letter to Michelle.. 19

A Fine Frenchman, an English Gentleman, and Me............ 22

A Younger Brother's Eulogy 25

NCCI at Gardner: An Oxymoron's Haven 29

What Does It All Mean? 34

'That One Wish' 38

Old Man – Future Me 40

An Open Letter Asking for Forgiveness 44

A Prince with a Golden Heart (by Paige M.L.) 49

A Call to Humanity.. 55

Finally, Gina 63

A Mother's Love.. 66

Reflection of Our Failures.. 68

'Maybe When I'm Gone' 73

A Small Church with a Bright Light.. 75

A Day of Reflection

First and foremost, let us shed the usual constraints of interaction facing us and allow me to correspond with you from the heart. I have been accused in the past of not being assertive enough; therefore, please allow me to do just that: be assertive.

We, as incarcerated men and women, share a deep despair represented by our very own lives within these walls – this HELL, if you will, that we come to know so well on such a personal level. We as prisoners share a tremendous pain in knowing that our collective burden is a byproduct of choices that we individually have made, which consequently have brought us to a place of great loneliness and despair, a despair that only those in our position can understand. Then, those who are innocent know with more clarity that this place can become even lonelier. It does not matter which prison you are serving out your sentence, nor which security level you are classified to, the feelings are the same.

We in general seem to forget about the importance of unity

and the spirit of community. We even forget, or perhaps chose to ignore, our collective obligation to others, to society and even to ourselves. Future generations are dependent on our actions.

In all my years of incarceration, I have shed many tears, expressed anger at many individuals and reached levels of heartache where I thought that I would be unable to go on living a healthy, productive life. These feelings changed once I became associated with a group of men who have taught me, through words and deeds, the importance of building emotional bridges that cross racial and adversarial divides. These men that I am referring to have a profound sense of common humanity, a sense of connection which I failed to see in the free world. Over time, they have become like family. They are my family. These men are all members of a small church within a small unit here at this facility. I have never been part of something so personal, where men are both loyal and encouraging. They are constantly putting the needs of others ahead of themselves. What will sustain this group, this family, over time is our commitment to each other. Through the years, I have seen many conflicts within prison walls, including conflicts about members of this group. I would say that most of the conflicts are the result of miscommunication, and only on occasion are the conflicts on substantial issues.

Being around these men has taught me the importance of standing up and being counted on issues relative to making this world a better place to live for all, not just for the selected and chosen ones.

If we are going to move forward in life in a positive manner, we need to stop making excuses for not wanting or being able to help the less fortunate members of our community. I wholeheartedly believe, and I see many examples around me, that even prisoners can make a difference. I believe that we have an obligation, especially those of us who owe society for our past actions, to leave this world a better place than how we came into it. (See "Changing the World From a Prison Cell.") We have to keep in mind what is important here: our lives and the lives of those we are in contact with on an everyday basis.

This is why it is vitally important to create a positive ripple effect in everything that we do. We should be channeling all our energy, not towards the destruction of each other, but toward helping each other grow and heal. Let us not forget that healing begins with us, in meeting our obligations of taking self-accountability for our very own actions.

Speaking from a prisoner's perspective, I say that we should recognize and embrace the fact that some of our past behaviors have caused terrible pain, not only to the victims of our actions and their families, to our communities and to society in general, but to our own families as well. We should further recognize and accept the fact that our incarceration does not automatically cancel out OUR SHARE OF RESPONSIBILITIES AND DEBT we owe to communities all around us.

We prisoners should be working together to best explore the impact of our crimes and actions and discuss the possibilities and opportunities for personal accountability and, further, for community responsibility. We need to come together on an intellectual level and encourage one another to take personal responsibility for our actions.

If there is one thing that I have learned from the men I alluded to earlier in this article, it is the importance of living a responsible life on a personal and profound level. Given that these men are LIFERS (by majority) and Christian men, I feel free from the restraints that we as prisoners put on each other.

Men and women that truly care and are not paying lip service cannot allow others to break their collective spirit. We have to lead others for the betterment of all the civilized world. We must allow others to learn from OUR collective mistakes, so that they do not repeat the same mistakes. Let us throw our future generations a lifeline, if you will.

With just a cursory look into our prisons, one can simply conclude that we do have resources that can assist in improving the quality of lives of all members of society. We have intellect. We have vast resources within our reach. Let us utilize this talent instead of playing the dramatic political games that we have grown accustomed to as of late.

If we say, and truly mean, that we have our future generations' future in mind, let us start to work towards our goals.

In conclusion, let me convey this: Let us stand up and be men and women of action, of principles and morals. Let us all do our part. Like many constructive and innovative developments within this country and in countries all around the world, it will require a farsighted and pioneering government that is prepared to resist potential opposition from the prevailing culture. We need state and federal professionals to become facilitators of a system that aims at offender accountability, reparation to society and the full participation of us all.

I now ask you this: Have I been assertive enough?

A Eulogy from a Son (and Friend)

I love you. These were the last words that my father spoke to me, said during our phone conversation of Sunday, February 20, 2005. It is my understanding that this was on the same day that he passed away.

I – Love – You!!! I would not trade those words for anything in this world. Many of you know my circumstances, of being in prison, yet I would gladly spend the rest of my life under these circumstances just to hear my father tell me once again just how much he loved me.

My father had a strong character. He was a man with few words. He was very protective of his family and had a knack for taking words such as knucklehead and turning them into loving words. When I first moved out of my parents' home and moved to Sturbridge, Massachusetts, he would often come by and check on me, using the excuse that he was doing this for "your mother, so that she would not worry." But, I knew he did it as much for himself. You see, my father was also a proud man and refused to show any signs of weakness. When I owned and operated my own business, he was often there, standing proud, talking with customers. He and I shared a love for baseball as well as being die-hard Dodgers fans.

Whenever I would speak about the love of my life, Michelle, he would ace me by telling me about his— my mother. I know that he loved her more than words could say. "**Ednooch**", as he would refer to her – her name is Edna. They made a good team. What a team! Through thick and thin, they never once let go of that love. The result (or by-product) of that love brought my brother Richard, my sisters Joann and Arlene and me into this world.

There are only a couple of things I can take comfort in, and they are easy to identify. For one, this past year my father and I became closer than ever. Our conversations were not just between a father and son but from one friend to another as well. Two, there was not one phone conversation that went by that he did not worry about me, wondering if I ate and expressing his love for me. Also, I take great pride in knowing that, yes, I am his son and I carry his name, **Celestino.**

My father never won a major award. He was not some celebrity, nor did he have a bridge named after him. Yet, he taught me so much. He taught me some fundamental truths I needed to know as I began this journey in life. He, together with my mother, taught my siblings and me the importance of living life with honesty, integrity and love towards others. He spoke about the fact that life is indeed short, at times tragic and always unpredictable. Though we may make plans and anticipate changes, not one of us knows what is ahead.

If there is one thing that my dad has taught me in his own way, it is that whatever the exigencies of history, we are most ourselves as lovers of freedom and keeping the spirit of America. Our daily acts of creation, untiring optimism and courage define us with far greater clarity and eloquence than do our moments of despair or feats of vengeance.

I personally plan to honor my father by my resolve to do the correct things in life. I have to, because, Dad,… **I LOVE YOU.**

(Written February 20, 2005, in tribute to my father, "Big Sal".)

'TO LOVE A WOMAN'

She's sitting there, thinking about their past,
about that love they once shared,
secretly wishing he held her within his arms,
and to show her again just how much he cared.
He held her, whenever she was afraid,
and missed her when she was away.
He protected her until he was gone,
and kept his feelings for her strong.
With those same rules of love in mind,
it kept their love going through time.
**Choir/Coro: There are joys two hearts, and only two,
can share. "To love a
woman" he once told me,
"is to love her passionately."**
One day my father said: "Son, your mother is the best thing
that ever happened to me."
We spoke as only two friends could.
He loved her 'til God took him home, just like we knew he

would.

He would send his love to her from beyond if he could,
and tell her: "You are the best thing to ever happen to me.
Our children and grandchildren are fruits of our love.
So always remember, my sweet, that you are and always will
be,
the pounding of my heart, even when there are no words
left to speak."

**Choir/Coro: There are joys two hearts, and only two,
can share. "To love a**
woman" he once told me,
"is to love her passionately."
Oh yes, she's sitting there thinking about their past,
about that love they once shared.
But she knows deep within her heart,
exactly just how much he cared.
To love a woman…
There are joys two hearts…
To love a woman…
and only two…
To love a woman…
can share
Oh, to love a woman
(Written for my parents on March 27, 2005)

Changing the World from a Prison Cell

I am sitting here, in this tiny compartment, my cell, which I call home. I have just finished reading Time Magazine's "The 100 Most Influential People" (May 2/ May 9, 2016 – double issue), for the third time. I am still in awe. I wholeheartedly believe each and every person that they spotlight is a representation of what is best in humanity – the best of the humane spirit. I am in wonder of certain individuals profiled more than others. In particular, I am drawn to **Nadia Murad**'s fierce advocacy and spirit – **Pricilla Chan** and **Mark Zuckerberg**'s extraordinary generosity – **Pope Francis'** embodiment of universal principles of kindness – **Charlize Theron**'s humanity – **Nikki Haley**'s compassion – **Donald Trump**'s non-conformist attitude – **Lin-Manuel Miranda**'s visionary spirit – and **Aung San Suu Kyi**'s humanitarian awareness.

All aforementioned individuals, along with others that

were written about, have done something to be recognized, a recognition for playing a positive role model for the rest of us. The world values action. From a personal viewpoint, they have each managed to remind me of what I have failed to do with my own life.

Through my years of incarceration, I have often thought about the things that I have not experienced in life, things that I missed out on. Most of all, I have thought about the important and vital things that I have not done.

You see, as I read about the **Nadia Murad**s of the world, I have come to the realization, or at the very least formed the opinion that we all, as members of humanity, are bound by an obligation to make this world a better place than when we came into it. How many times within our own lives have we thought that life itself was too short, that, before we have finished what we have in mind, we have become old and feeble, as if the Grim Reaper was knocking at our door? It is human nature. We seek out answers for the uncertainties in life. This is when we need tenacity and audacity to lead us.

I have come to believe with every fiber of my being that, if you have the courage of your convictions, you must stand up and be counted. There is this maxim, this ancient principle of law: **"qui tacit cons entire"**, which means "to be silent is to be content". There is too much pain and suffering in the world today to simply remain silent and/or not to take action. All around us are people in need, and sometimes we have to set aside our own feelings and agendas to help them. I have learned that the most precious things we can pass down to our children, to future generations, is our love and a compassionate spirit towards others. How easy it is to be engrossed in our own concerns and forget that someone right next to us might need a simple act of kindness: a prayer, a word of comfort, a hug or simply a hello – some form of recognition. I believe that we should be of service to one another.

Some may say that I am just a prisoner. Some may point out the fact that I am in prison serving a life sentence, and they might say that I have the gall, the temerity even, to believe in these things "only after the fact", as if it being in prison for life was the end of the world. But, NO! I do not believe this to be true, nor will I entertain the idea that I cannot do something positive and productive to enrich or enlighten someone else's life.

My three decades of incarceration have made me see life very differently. Something within me has been altered. All the inner workings and mechanisms have been irreparably changed, in an optimistic way. I have learned that no matter how precarious our circumstances become, we need to battle through them. I have learned that what matters most in life is knowing that love was, and still is, all mine to give, without strings or expectations.

Subsequently, at this moment, I am desperately – helplessly – longingly – quietly – and patiently crying, from deep within the bowels of my heart. I have come face to face with and experienced some of life's rawest emotions. I have witnessed firsthand humility supplicating with tears. I have heard wisdom urging her solemn plea, and due to this experience I believe a metamorphosis has developed within me.

Putting these words on paper today, given the trials and tribulations that I have endured, is a matter of astonishment as well as gratitude. Gratitude that we live in a country that allows its citizens, even a prisoner serving out a life sentence, the opportunity to speak his mind and express himself fully. I am able to throw my thoughts hastily and imperfectly together, simply hoping to convey to anyone the importance of creating a positive ripple effect around themselves. We should all be taking the "What can I do to make another person's life better" approach.

Just because I will be dying within these walls, a matter of choice and principle, amputated from the world for the most part, it does not mean that I can not do my part in making the world around me better. I can mentor a younger prisoner, especially one that will ultimately be released from prison, into becoming a productive member of society. I can show him the importance of living life with morals and compassion, a life committed to something with virtues, and the importance in thriving to do better each and every day. I can show him the importance of cultivating positive ideas and a new attitude to better sharpen certain traits such as kindness and integrity, humor and sensibility. I can lead him by example by showing him that it is a matter of choice, that when we face devastating experiences in life, we can define them either in terms of despair or hope. It is important to show him that though we must sail on into an uncertain future, we must always remember to let the rich colors of love, joy, peace, patience, kindness and self-control shine through and not allow the negative thoughts of our plight deter us in doing positive things. I would remind him that during the journey we take in life, there will be regrets, even regrets about the journey itself, but not the destination, especially if our destination is full of love and fulfillment.

Furthermore, I can use my position and voice, being an experienced "Jailhouse lawyer", to do things. I can "Litigate", "Educate", "Legislate" and/or "Adjudicate" in a manner that would bring awareness to prisoners' plight. I can write letters, open letters to the community, conveying the importance of forgiveness and redemption. I can direct other prisoners to donate money to various causes, especially if it will create and/or offer some atonement. I can even write a book expressing positive thoughts.

I do understand the fact that it is easy to lose sight in a culture riddled with immorality. Our lives too may seem to be in ruins. Troubles of our own making and conflicts we cannot avoid may leave us too devastated, without an ounce of fight left, or it sure would seem that way. I know all of this. I speak from experience, but we have to find a way to tap into our inner strength to somehow transform ourselves. Instead of being agents of condemnation, we should be ambassadors of love and mercy. Above all, we should be cheerleaders of a world where anyone can achieve anything they set their minds to if they never lose hope.

For those like me, that have lived a life haunted by past wrongdoings and misjudgments, we have to keep in mind that tomorrow is a new day with no mistakes. Today is the day to begin anew. Let us stop focusing on the disappointments of yesterday or the uncertainties of tomorrow. Let us enjoy the gift that has been given to us today.

So yes, from a prison cell, I too can make a difference. Thanks to the good people of Time Magazine for finding a way to convey to us all the importance and power of influence. Thank you for reminding me that my bloodline yearns for freedom, but my heart-line is tied to the world of the incarcerated, especially those innocent prisoners in Massachusetts and around the globe.

CIRCLE OF CARING

When I was growing up, I remember my parents telling my siblings and me, more teaching us a lesson if anything, about the importance of allowing life to shape our character in a meaningful and profound manner. They would say: "Son, every morning, as you look into the mirror while preparing and fixing yourself to go out into the world, ask yourself what new lesson life will teach you today…." Then they would go on: "…and at the end of the day, while you are preparing for bed, you better have an answer or else you've wasted the lesson for that day."

Of course, I have wasted thousands of these opportunities to learn. That is, until the day my dad passed away and those aforementioned words came rushing back into my life. Since then, February 20, 2005, with God's grace, I have lived by this motto: Every day, I search out the truth and meaning in life and what lessons I can learn from them.

Now: What truths have I found during my search? Well, for one thing, there are thousands of examples of good to be found on an everyday basis, if we are attentive to them, that is. I have come to cherish the little things in life that we generally take for granted.

I now realize that there is a circle of caring all around me. At times I cannot see it, but it is there, made up of friends and family who love me and know how difficult the life of a prisoner is. They are there to convey to us that we can take comfort and find strength in knowing that we are thought of, cared about, and that despite our plight, we are not alone. God reminds us that we are loved.

As we go through difficult times in our lives, such things can cause us to ask: "Why did this happen to me?" But if we search for the truth, we know that we do not have to search long to see God's grace all around us, and if we are trusting in Him, we never need to ask: "How could He let this happen?" No matter what circumstances we go through, God may choose never to reveal all His reasons to us, but He has certainly revealed His unwavering character.

His character assures us that He never makes mistakes, is never uncaring, and that He never separates Himself from our needs. He understands us.

In that same spirit, we find a circle of caring around us in the form of selfless volunteers who take time from their own lives to simply convey to us the positive things in life, to show us its goodness and God's love for us.

God sends us these individuals to convey to us that, yes, He believes in us. If, as earthly parents, many of us root for our children to do well in life, and we confirm said desires in addition to telling them that we believe in them, imagine how God feels about His children. He believes in the things that are important to us: that we can accomplish anything that we set out to do, as long as we do it for His glory; that we have talents and the wisdom to use them well; that we have what it takes to overcome obstacles, with His help, and grow from every experience life brings our way; and that we will always be faithful to our friends and family and to the values that have shaped our philosophy – our courage, compassion, strength of character and the goodness in us.

God also sends us His Spirit to be by our side, to comfort us, guide us, protect us and encourage us. He instills His Spirit profoundly within us, who is there to be by our side, watching out for us in all the things we do, reminding us to keep believing in brighter days, finding ways for our wishes, prayers and dreams to come true, giving us hope in a future as certain as the sun comes up and giving us the strength of serenity as our guide. God is our guiding light and our shield.

This is why we, as human beings, especially as God's children, have love, comfort and courage built within us. We only need to tap into those gifts. We have all been given gifts with the hope that we would share them with others. We have an obligation to others around us to assist them, catch them if they fall, encourage their dreams, inspire their happiness and hold their hand and help them through it all.

In all our days, our lives are always changing. Tears come along as well as smiles. Yet, we have one constant things to lean on, and that is God's love for us.

Remember, along the roads we travel, the miles are a thousand times more lovely than lonely simply because of our belief in Him. All we have to do is stop and listen to His voice in the form of the wind, see Him in the form of other people's faces and feel Him in the form of our love towards others. We must simply love as He does.

In conclusion, allow me to say this: Let us be thankful for anyone who plays a part in enriching our lives. Remember, it is a gift of God to us in the form of a circle of caring individuals that are all around us. Thank you for playing a role in this wonderful and joyous life and for giving a hand to the less fortunate: the poor, the sick, the lonely and, yes, prisoners.

Let us be there for one another. Life is too short and fragile, but it is all too beautiful as well.

A Letter to Michelle

I have heard it said countless times in my life that Time heals all wounds. I believe those words were uttered by someone who never experienced a broken heart. When you left me, and with good reason, it took me a very long time to get over you. I do not blame you and not once have I hated you for leaving me. What the hell, I was immature at the time and was not equipped to be in a relationship with you, nor anyone else for that matter.

Still, it took twenty-four long years to get over you. Not until Paige entered my life was I finally able to let you go. You played such an immense and profound role in my life. I wasted so much time dwelling on my loss instead of living my life.

Perhaps it was due to my incarceration and the hell that I lived because of it. Perhaps it was because we never, at least on my part, found closure. I never said goodbye to you in a proper manner. My time in prison made me bitter, yet I managed to survive. I went through a metamorphosis and I finally became the man that you needed, only much too late. In fact, after my relationship with you, I attempted to start anew with others, particularly with Gina, only, due to my immaturity, to hurt her as well.

I failed you, I know. Every relationship after you was doomed before it started, simply because of my broken life. I allowed my failed relationship with you, coupled with personal and tragic events in my life, to dictate how I treated others. In fact, if the truth be told, I was doing something that was not fair to others. I started to measure them to you, in which, given that I held you up on a pedestal, was extremely unfair to them.

The very last time that we spoke, I needed so badly to tell you things, but I was not, due to circumstances, able to. I remember, towards the end of our relationship, this song came on the radio: "It Must Have Been Love", by Roxette. I was standing outside your car, and you pointed to the radio and asked me if I had heard this song, and then you asked me to listen to it. A few weeks later, I was driving and I heard it again, and once it came to the part where the singer said "It must have been love, but it's over now", that is when the realization hit me like a ton of bricks. My life would never be the same. The trajectory it would take would make me a different man, a cynical and bitter man — not towards you, but towards myself. I hated myself for losing you.

There are things that have happened to me since that are somewhat related to you, which I write in my other book: "If I Had Only… Lived". It is a personal account of my life and things I needed to tell you, but this too was not meant to be.

You are and always will be my great and true love, though Paige has showed me that in life the heart does have room for two great loves. You represent my past, while she represents my present.

For whatever it is worth, I pray to God that He has blessed you in life and that the road you chose has given you a beautiful and full life. I pray that you have seen your dreams come true and that you have beautiful children and a wonderful significant other. I pray that everything you put your mind to has brought you all the joy that life brings. Life is too short to do what I have done for many years, dwelling on the past instead of living life. I buy into this now: Revisit the past in order to best live it.

Thank you for the wonderful memories and the love we once shared. May God bless you. And I do apologize for taking a long time to finally grow up.

A Fine Frenchman, an English Gentleman, and Me

I have been incarcerated for far too many years. During this time I have met all sort of characters. When you take into account the number of prisoners, correctional guards, administrators, maintenance workers and all sort of staff members and volunteers that I have met and associated with, well, that is a lot, especially given the fact that I have traveled through all the adult male prisons in Massachusetts, some as many as four times over. I say all of this to make this point: I have met many good people.

If I were to pick my top five individuals that I have met, it would be an extremely hard task for me to do. But I will say this much: There are two men in my life that have demonstrated to me the fact that there are still good people around, even in a prison environment. But what makes these two individuals extremely special is that they, like me, are serving life sentences.

In prison, one must choose "friends" very carefully. There

is a cynical vibe one automatically employs when dealing with individuals. Yet, not only do I consider these two individuals "friends", but if the truth be told, they are my family.

J.R. (Jacques Robidoux) (the Frenchman) and Neil Entwistle (the Englishman) have proven to me that there are individuals that come into your life to enrich it. I have identified these two men as blessings from God Himself. You see, our Lord has a knack for putting people in our lives for various reasons. Each and every day, we three, the Frenchman, the Englishman and I, seek out one another to pray, spend time together, break bread and to converse about the ways we as Christians and Godly men can improve the lives of our fellow prisoners and their families.

I have seen and experienced selflessness before. I have seen this in my parents in reference to me and my siblings. I have seen it in various others towards people that matter to them. But to see it and feel it inside a prison, well, it is a whole different level. These two are the most selfless individuals I have ever met. They inspire me to do my best. They have demonstrated to me the importance of creating relationships based on Godly principles.

I lost my brother Richard some eight years ago (see "**A Younger Brother's Eulogy**"). But God has brought me, right here in prison, not one, but two brothers to remind me about the things that I need to do on my quest of changing the world from a prison cell. (See "**Changing the World From a Prison Cell**".)

These men have been there for me, especially in a year full of uncertainties during the COVID-19 Pandemic, in a manner that my brother Richard would have done. Our God continues to prove to me, via these two men, and others who share our beliefs, that it does not matter where we call home if we are surrounded by caring and loving individuals, individuals that love unconditionally and in a manner that is important for the betterment of us as humans.

Whenever I think about these men, how they give of themselves without limit and the fact that they are both doing life sentences, it so astonishes me. They are constantly conveying to all those around them by words and deeds the importance of living life in a way that enriches others in all aspects of their lives.

I was under the belief that longevity in prison was attained only if you epitomized physical strength and were ready to meet whatever challenges came along as a person who oozed machismo. The tougher you were, or at least the tougher exterior you portrayed, the better position you were in to handle obstacles, at least within the prison context. I was wrong. J.R. and Neil have demonstrated to me that they in fact are strong and independent men simply because of their faith and how they have this "Let Go, Let God" attitude. There is nothing that deters these men away from their faith in our Lord. I have about the same amount of time in prison as these two men combined, yet they seem to have figured out something that I failed to do: When you are a man of faith, of good moral character, and have a wholehearted belief in your Maker, there are no circumstances and no person that can be detrimental to you, as long as you trust in God for everything.

I love and respect these men. They have earned my admiration in ways that few have in all my years of incarceration. That is saying something. For the rest of my life, I am indebted to them for teaching me the true measure of a man.

This chapter is dedicated to these two men, my brothers in Christ.

A Younger Brother's Eulogy

On the day my brother Richard was born, he came into a modest home and proceeded to be a blessing to my parents: Celestino, my dad, or Big Sal as many would call him; and Edna, my beautiful and loving mother. Richard would spend the rest of his life being a blessing to not only my parents, but to every person that he touched. He was a special human being, and one I am proud to call my brother.

I was born the second child of four siblings, and at first I had a healthy sibling rivalry with him. No matter what I did or what I accomplished, I would always seem to somehow come up short. You see, he would remind me that I was number two, the younger of the brothers. Being the oldest, he was the first to reach various milestones before me. He was the first to reach "pre-teen" status. I remember once I reached that, he was quick to remind me: "Brother, I am no longer a 'pre-teen', I am a teenager now." This rivalry would play out in all aspects of our lives, so yes, at first, this would bother me. Eventually, he would go on to accomplish many feats and milestones ahead of me. As we grew older, I not only came to accept this, I came to cherish it as well.

Whenever I think about my brother, I cannot help but to think about the endless selfless acts that he did, making sure that everything he did was for the betterment of the family.

He was the epitome of a true and loyal Mama's Boy, and he often spoke proudly about this – making sure that my mother was always as comfortable as possible. She was with him when he passed away, and I am sure that this is the most comforting fact of all.

He, being the oldest sibling, made sure to take it upon himself to be very protective of my younger sisters (Joann and Arlene) and me. Whenever I would tell him that I felt as though our cousin Raymond was like another brother to me, not once did he feel jealous or threatened. On the contrary, he would tell me never to lose that feeling and would go on to tell me how important that feeling was. That was the type of person he was. He was a man of integrity. He represented all things good and was a man that anyone could have molded their lives after.

He has come to represent to me a true model, a man that I will always make reference to in a positive and loving manner.

After Dad's death, my brother Richard assumed responsibility of being our family's leader – our rock and our strength. In fact, from the moment that he gave me the news of Dad's passing, through his own fight with cancer, which ultimately claimed his life, he would show me why he was such a special human being. He was a man that loved his family profoundly.

Whenever he would speak about family, it was always with a loving and kind heart. Whether speaking about cousin Madeline (one of his all-time favorite persons – ever), or any other member of our family, he would always express that family was the most important and vital thing in life.

In everything that he did, he put family first. If I spend the rest of my life giving just ten percent of what he gave towards the betterment of our family, I would be assured of enriching the lives of each and every member of my family.

September 2, 2013 will always represent to me the day our Lord asked for my brother to join Him. It will always be the day I lost my brother, yet, the day Heaven gained an angel, a special angel, an advocate representing all that is good in this world.

If I close my eyes, a flash of beautiful memories come to mind. Words cannot express the profound loss I feel at this moment, yet, I take great comfort in knowing that he is in Heaven with our Lord, surrounded by Dad and all those that have passed before him. I imagine my Dad waiting by Heaven's gate for his oldest son, waiting there to hug him and welcome him there and to tell him that he does not have to suffer anymore.

Yes, he touched my life in a manner that I can honestly say, without hesitation, "Brother, I am extremely proud to be number two to you".

If only I could somehow be half the man that he represented, then I would be a man of whom people would say: "There goes a man of integrity, of substance, of honor."

I love you Brother, and although you are not physically here with us, you will always live within my heart. If my words mean anything, they represent the immense love that I have for you, and yes, you are and are always going to be #1 in my heart. I will gladly be #2 to your #1 because you taught me so much in life. You took the teachings of our parents and made a blueprint to be followed. I will do my best on the rest of this journey called life to make you proud of your little brother. Tell Dad and the rest of ours that we will meet up someday. Perhaps you will be waiting for your little brother by Heaven's gate, to remind him that yes, you were the first one there.

I love you Bro – Your little brother Sal.

NCCI at Gardner:
An Oxymoron's Haven

Disclaimer: I wrote this article while I was engaged in a very bitter and hostile battle against prison officials at the facility in 2017. This resulted in them moving me three times to three different facilities. Now that I have recommitted my life to Jesus, my fight for justice remains but I no longer harbor bitterness against them.

Upon entering the North Central Correctional Institution, a medium-security facility within the Town of Gardner, Massachusetts, one will quickly conclude that this place is much different than any other prison, at least here in Massachusetts anyway.

You see, if you stood outside these prison gates looking in, you would say that it is a somewhat beautiful, peaceful sort of place. It oozes tranquility, at least as far as prisons go, with its trees, many colorful flower beds, well-tended landscapes, birds flying all around, squirrels being hand fed, not to mention the vegetable garden.

Yes, it is fair to say, based on appearance, that this facility is in fact different. It would tempt any prisoner to want to retire at this facility and escape the mundane nature of prison life.

I first came to deal with the Massachusetts Department of Correction on October 25, 1990. Since then, I have done my term and served my sentence in every adult male facility at one time or the other, sometimes multiple times. I have officially been adjudicating and/or litigating matters within our judicial system since the very beginning of my incarceration. I have dealt with all facets of law: Civil – Criminal – Probate – Immigration – Constitutional – Contracts – Administrative, et cetera. I have dealt with every level within said system, from the local District Trial Court through the United States Supreme Court, for either myself personally or in assistance of other prisoners. I am referred to as a "Jailhouse lawyer". I have sat on the Board of Directors of Prison Legal Services (formerly Massachusetts Correctional Legal Services) since 2001. I do not come from a long line of miscreants. I am from a family that fights for whatever is correct and just. If my late older brother Richard were here with me today, he would remind me that "It is better to champion a losing cause that you believe in than to keep your silence and risk nothing." This is the type of outlook we were raised on. My motto is: Tall mountains may be harder to climb than a hill, but the view from the top is always worth it. This is why I aim, despite being incarcerated, for the tallest mountain.

With my experience and upbringing comes some knowledge, and when I step back away from the aforementioned trees and the birds and really take a good long look at this facility, I start to see things for what they truly are. Much is not quite right; indeed, much is amiss.

Through the years, I have dealt with different types of administrators. Some come across as tyrants, while others choose to employ the quid pro quo approach. But this place is much different. It is much more sinister. The prisoner who has the knowledge, the know-how, can see that the inner workings of this facility do not follow the Constitutional norm.

You see, the prison officials here are constantly breaking the law. They blatantly break the law in so many ways and sit back daring anyone to say one word. "Go ahead, rock the boat" as they say. Once a person starts to question things, well, they quickly come to realize that there is something rotten in Denmark – you are not in Kansas anymore.

Once you have been a target, once they believe that you may be the cause of "John Q. Public" being made aware of their wrong doings, or if they get the hint that any type of complaint against them is forthcoming, well, they start to employ a degree of tactics, "Forth-with, if not sooner," as my friend Paul likes to say.

The administrators here, the officials of this prison, never get their hands dirty. They use some intermediate agents, their minions, to start sending subliminal messages. They find ways to employ their Kangaroo Court system. They subvert illegal tactics, surmise charges against you, obstruct justice and keep you incommunicado from people on the outside. They employ all their department bureaucracies in a manner which creates a smoke screen in order to camouflage the truth in things. They break, or at least attempt to break, your support system. They start using the "Fox guarding the hen house" approach. They retaliate against you. They slander you. They tenaciously harass you. They gossip about you to other prisoners, hoping that they turn against you. They exploit the situation. They become a terrible pest and nuisance, thereby going against the crux of our rehabilitation. They try to keep you as vulnerable as possible. They destruct and vandalize your possessions. They "lose" vital documents.

There is nothing that they will not do, absolutely nothing, if it means that taxpayers will not find out about things within this "nice community of prisoners." Shoot, they even have cut down the trees within this facility in an inconspicuous manner, in a place where it should be protected by the National Historical Society.

In fact, a case could be made for this place to be the most preposterous, inconspicuous place within the Massachusetts Department of Correction (DOC), and that is saying something, given the fact that the DOC is full of less-than-professional individuals.

How do you stop ignorance when the ignorant person does not seem to care? If you try to implore to their common sense, well, you would have to find it first. One look at their Curriculum Vitae is like seeing one of Tex Avery's Looney Tunes. Anyone with half a brain would be completely stunned by the droll of their actions. Try to figure out a way to escape the tedium and misery of being in a place full of idiocy. Trust me, I tried.

If you try communicating all of this to the leaders of the Department of Correction, or even to the Governor of Massachusetts himself, Charles "Charlie" Baker, you come to conclude that they have managed to condition themselves like ostriches, sticking their hands in the sand, or up their asses for that matter, whenever problems arise.

Their collective actions have given me more audacity than common sense, for I keep on and will continue to "Rock the boat."

Well, what does someone like me do with all of this? I am a nonconformist, a recalcitrant of the DOC; so, bring it on you Pusillanimous imbeciles.

WHAT DOES IT ALL MEAN?

When I was growing up, my mother would tell me a story: Every morning in Africa, a gazelle (a small swift antelope) would wake up and know that in order to survive one more day, it had better be ready to outrun a predator, such as a lion. Meanwhile, every morning a lion would be waiting, ready to pounce on his prey because its survival was at stake as well. Survival of the fittest.

Applying the aforementioned analogy, if you will, we can liken it to the lives of prisoners ("…in order to survive…") and the financially driven Correctional Industries ("…Ready to pounce…") of this country.

If one were to examine a prisoner's heart, not a cursory examination but a profound one, one would see that the average prisoner is not the evil person that he is commonly believed to be, but is instead a by-product of a broken heart. At one time or another, he or she became the by-product of a broken life. Said prisoner has most likely been mistreated and misunderstood, and the odds are that they have been taken advantage of, in one form or another, most of their lives. These things are most likely the chief malady and source of all their grief. Prisoners are in a very vulnerable position, whether by their own misguided doing or not, and poverty and the lack of knowledge play a major role as well. All these are characteristics of a potential prey.

On the other side, the correctional institutions are the quintessential predators. They seem to go on their daily lives with that blindness which seems to be the unvarying characteristic of tyrants, trying to take advantage of the weaker individuals. If you stand back and study the scenery, you could almost smell the smoke of a profound animosity between them – prey and predator – each playing a role of and striving to become a survivor.

Today, it may seem that our collective heads are in the lion's mouth, but we may have a glimmering ray of hope. I believe with every fiber of my being that the pendulum of time is swinging in our direction. I believe that the propagators of these institutions and their successors are starting to lose momentum. I believe that they are becoming weak, sensual and rapacious in that they are losing sight of the fact that we are in dire need of surviving.

Just like in Africa, the gazelles have learned that their best chance of survival is to start running early, and in a pack. We prisoners too, undoubtedly, are cultivating new attitudes. As a result of being put in a position of having to survive in our present plight, we prisoners are taking a different approach than of those of past generations. Gone are the days of work stoppages and riots, at least in this Commonwealth. I believe that we prisoners are attempting to change our conditions in an articulate manner. I believe that we have developed perseverance. I believe that we have developed intellectual strength. I believe that we have developed, in general, a tenacity of purpose and other attributes, despite being labeled and being treated as "malcontents."

Let us be totally honest here, this is a played-upon sociological interpretation as a result of a propaganda created and disseminated by those same predators that I have alluded to. I believe that we have vital skills to supplement each other. I believe that there is a metamorphosis happening in prisoners as of late. I believe that prisoners are starting to see the light.

What we need to do, though, is better define a prisoner's role and place it in its proper perspective, particularly in terms of the current social, economic and political upheaval in America today. This topic has caused a great deal of provocation, misunderstanding and misinterpretation. We need to stop constantly fighting amongst ourselves, looking for all things negative in each other. We need to understand that while doing these negative things, we take our eyes off the prize, off survival, and thereby give the adversary more of an advantage.

We need to stop taking the dilly-dallying, pussy-footing, compromising approach to our plight. We need to force (non-violently) our government, perhaps via our collective supporters' votes and/or voices, to change its conduct. Their conduct currently is hideous and revolting. We need to understand, educate, remind and/or inform ourselves of the fact that laws of a nation, yes, even here in America, especially here in America, are more due to the public's misunderstood sentiments and its civilization than of its promises of freedom and human rights. We need to find a way to implore the social, political and economical conditions of all Americans.

In essence: **What Does It All Mean?** We need to look at

the principles in all things advocating humane compassion, human injustice and human rights. We need to stand by those principles, be true to them on all occasions, in all places, against all foes, at whatever cost and not sacrifice our dignity and honor or our integrity in order to accomplish this.

Let us survive.

'THAT ONE WISH'

If I was granted 'That One Wish',
What would it be?
Would I ask The Heavens, To Return My Son,
Dad or a lost loved one, back to me?
I would close my eyes and search deep within my heart,
And it comes clear to me – 'That One Wish'
Has to come from profoundly within my heart.
Some may ask for fortune, others for fame.
Some may pray for freedom, others seek eternal love,
But one thing that is clear to me,
And that's that 'That One Wish'
Has to come from profoundly within my heart.
I can ask for the chance to correct my past,
I may even ask for a future as bright as the sun,
But let's be honest here – 'That One Wish'
Has to come from profoundly within my heart.
So let's get one thing clear here.
I live for today – not for yesterdays,

Nor for tomorrows,
And today you're in my life,
Giving me the chance to love and fantasize about what is important,
And that is that you are here to share my life and my dreams,
All while enriching my life.
So yes, 'That One Wish' has been answered, it is you my love.
Written on July 30, 2013
Dedicated to Paige M.L.

OLD MAN – FUTURE ME

If I close my eyes, it does not hurt quite so bad. Reaching backwards over the years I have asked myself: Where have the years gone? I am startled by the vividness with which I can recall when I first came into prison. The sights and sounds are engraved profoundly deep within me. I cannot escape them.

I recall the long lines for everything, the body language so different from men in the free world. The majority of men had their heads bowed as they shuffled towards grimy prison workshops. I thought to myself: "These are men devoid of all human feelings", and I promised myself never to be like them. I thought to myself that I was different than they. I believed that their stare was peculiar to the imprisoned, only to those that were "guilty" and not for someone like myself. I recall seeing the majority of men attempting to hide their true feelings. Some attempted by taking advantage of the weaker, while some simply avoided as much human contact as possible. Nevertheless, they all had that look: eyes fixed straight ahead, staring, yet unseeing, lost in deep thought about other, happier times. Whether it was thinking about a loved one, perhaps their children, or a mom or dad, or some great love that they lost due to circumstances in life, their look conveyed to me the pain they carried. Some, like me, walked around with a broken heart, missing family, and wishing for the return of a long-lost love.

I saw the hurt and humiliation on the faces of the young, whether prisoner or visitor. Any time that I would go out into that lifeless visitation room to see a loved one, I could feel what every other prisoner at one time or another would feel: the feeling that though one would sit only inches from the visitor, we would be a world apart, separated by heartache and misery. I would feel a wave of remorse rise up in my throat for my part in dealing them the pain of being in prison and in not being there at any family and friends' gatherings – every wedding, funeral, birthday, holiday, et cetera. For many of us, we would see time travel through time. For the imprisoned, time felt as if it stood still at the same time. In our hearts and mind, we would feel as though ages and years would stay put waiting for us, while in actuality life moved on without us.

We in prison are conditioned to see life differently. We approach time as though we were trapped in a cemetery for the living. We are alive, yet dead. We live in a kaleidoscope of emotions: fear, sorrow, anger, frustration, emptiness, hurt and loneliness.

I refused to believe that the impersonality of prison could smother me too in anonymity, or fill my eyes with that vacant, unseeing, dead stare. Yet, despite all my efforts, I too somehow have changed. Perhaps not as extreme as others, but still I am not the same man that I was yesteryear. In retrospect, it is not totally bad. My advantage is that I have kept my emotions raw and alive. I have written down my thoughts and have dealt with my feelings in a manner that is positive. Yes, I for a very long time existed in this world rather than lived it, but I learned how to deal with all of this in a profound manner. Now I come to deal with the reality of life, my life, my circumstances, my plight. I now see there is no escape from the total inevitability of despair and hopelessness awaiting some, while others only seem to accept it, and to some degree welcome it.

I do recognize that this despair and hopelessness that sometimes suffocates individual prisoners, if not attended to, could easily reach the very bowels of a person, thereby making it impossible for them to escape the permeation. But, I do believe in the old prison adage: Do Time and Do Not Allow Time To Do You.

Most if not all prisoners surrender to a despair of prison life. I do understand this, but I also seem to have figured out that this is true only if you allow it to control you. The capitulation comes sooner in some than in others, and more subtly; sometimes it creeps stealthily and secretly into the nature of a person, as it did to me. But there will come a day when you awaken and realize that you are indeed changing. You see the reflection in the mirror as something unbelievably unrecognizable about you. You come to recognize that you have become another one of those shuffling, snarling and half-maddened men called convicts, going through the motions and not living the productive life that you thought you would at the beginning of this journey called life.

Once you survive this prison world, you come to realize that you have become a man apart from his fellow men, a stranger to the world around you, and even more foreign to the world outside these prison walls.

Long ago, I was caught up in the dreary monotony of prison life. Now, as the years pile on, my time in this world seems to get shorter at a fast clip. I may add that I have come to accept the fact that even prison life has passed by me. And so, I come to a conundrum: Do I give up trying to live a positive life, or do I do what my heart yearns for, and that is: How Do I Change This World from a Prison Cell?

I came into prison a young man, violent and uncontrolled, so they said. I became a victim of my own dark passions. I was part of the era that spawned men of action. I was part of the changing of the guard, so to speak. I came into prison at a time when we challenged authority when they blatantly violated the law. Due to my litigations, coupled with my attitude towards the authorities, especially those that treated prisoners as animals, prison life seemed to swallow me up. I found my own kind of a special hell. I was targeted for having the audacity to challenge things that were amiss.

Unfortunately, due to the aforementioned, I began for many years to nurture a profound hatred for the tangible aspects of my own private little hell. At some point, I started savoring each day, remembering the past, praying, hoping and looking forward to the day when I would once more become a part of a world, even though it was changing ever so rapidly towards concepts that I have never experienced.

One thing my life in prison has taught me, for good or evil, is that I have come to represent society's treatment of the less fortunate. I have come to put society's dignity on display for all to see. I represent the bone marrow of the cancer called prison.

AN OPEN LETTER ASKING FOR FORGIVENESS

If you are reading this letter, it may be because, at one time or another, I have hurt you, whether directly or indirectly, and I humbly ask, no plea, for your forgiveness. It is with the most profound regret and humility that I send this message, not only in hope of receiving forgiveness, but perhaps of also being furnished with the opportunity to convey to you things about myself that consequently and unfortunately drove my actions, that may have resulted in me hurting you or, perhaps, someone dear to you. Whether or not the results were a direct or proximate cause of any harm does not change the results. If this letter reaches you, it is because the message was meant to reach you, touch you and convey to you that, due to my actions in the past, I've had to endure some great ordeal in which I have been more than deserving. Yet, I plea for the opportunity for redemption.

You see, people in pain don't always see things as clearly

as they should, and sometimes a lot of negative emotions accompany us such as frustration, despair, fear and doubt. People ruled by these emotions will often make poor decisions, and because of this innocent people inevitably get hurt. I have acted without stopping to think about the consequences. I have made some poor choices, and for that I am sorry, so painfully sorry.

I have learned, perhaps much too late, that on the road of life crucial decisions are like intersections that call for us to choose which way to go. If we barrel through the road we pick, it may lead to regret and heartache. I have also learned that when we act or speak, a chain reaction ripples outward to affect the entire community. One small action can have a widespread effect, for good or bad.

Some people say that a person's success in life is measured by their actions – by how many friends they have – by whether or not they have a significant other – by how much wealth they have accumulated – by whether they have children to carry on their name and/or heritage, their legacy – and, once they have departed from this life, by how many people show up at their funeral. Under these measures, considering that I threw it all away, I guess that I am a complete failure. These are the consequences of my actions. I have come to accept this. People often say that love is the essence of a full and wonderful life. What happens when there is no love in a person's life?

I have made, as I mentioned, some poor decisions in my life, and ultimately I have hurt others, but I am not an evil person. Many of the choices and decisions I have made were some of the hardest that any human being would have had to make. I made many bad decisions simply because I was haunted by the past. In fact, the odds are that at the time I made said decisions, it probably was at a time in my life where I was simply existing – going aimlessly through life – shuffling along, instead of actually living my life the way I should have. I simply could not function because I was, and perhaps to a certain extent will be until I take my last breath, under conviction of and dwelling on guilt over past wrongdoings. Vacillating trust in others may have contributed to my making wrong and harsh decisions with dire consequences to myself that also proved detrimental to those I love. Pain and anger within me vied for dominance.

I attribute two specific things in my life as being the main forces driving me and my decisions, both for good and bad: 1) A broken heart, and 2) Being blinded due to a particular incident too painful to put into words. The combination of both these things only served to poison me. They haunted me and subsequently made me hate life and everything about it. In fact, hatred in me lived like a parasite for far too long (well over twenty years). It fed off me and grew bigger and uglier and stronger each and every day until it filled itself completely. It was not until Paige entered my life that I was able to love again. (See following article, **"A Prince with a Golden Heart"** – written by Paige M.L. about me.) Paige gave me the gift of loving again.

People may wonder: Why write an open letter? The truth is that I need to make amends to so many people and offer some atonement. I believe that the individuals that need to fully understand how remorseful I have become are the same people that I have come to wholeheartedly believe want to know this. I cannot seem to be able to forgive myself until I have the assurance that I, at the very least, tried to rectify my past actions.

I do understand that the passing of time has not salved the

wounds that I have inflicted, whether directly or indirectly. I fully accept this fact and understand that I cannot change it either, unfortunately.

One cursory look at my life and the romantics may call it a love story while the cynics may call it a tragedy. When all is said and done, it does not matter. It all involves a majority part of my life and the ultimate life I chose to follow.

I have lived, for the most part, an extremely lonely life. I fell deeply in love at nineteen, knowing even back then that nothing in the world would ever compare to that one single moment when I first kissed the girl of my dreams and knowing that my love for her would last forever. I lost her, losing the greatest part of who I was. I took decades to overcome this loss, and only, as I alluded to above, with Paige's help. You see, I am a man who loves deeply (which is a blessing), but I am also a man who loves forever (which may be a curse).

On top of all that I had endured in life, life itself furnished me with events that changed the course of my life even further. I was put in prison despite being innocent. I became a broken man, only to experience greater pain (both physically and psychologically) and eventually lose the rest of myself.

I have experienced the fact that youth offers the promise of happiness (I was a very happy young man), but life also offers the realities of grief (while incarcerated I have lost twenty-four family and friends, including the two most influential men in my life: my father and best friend (See "**A Eulogy from a Son (and Friend)**"); and my brother (See "**A Younger Brother's Eulogy**").

It has been a long and lonely journey. That young man left home to embark on a life full of promise, only to go through hell on earth. Yet, I do not make excuses for my actions. I

have to hold myself accountable for my actions. I am sorry for inflicting any pain towards you or a member of your family.
Please forgive me.

A Prince with a Golden Heart (by Paige M.L.)

I was born in Dublin, Ireland. Both my parents were born there as well. I was raised on the outskirts of London, England – the countryside – and finished my higher education in America.

When I was a little girl, I dreamed that a knight in white shining armor would protect me if I were ever in any sort of danger. Then, growing up into a young lady, I would often fantasize that someday I would meet and eventually fall in love with a prince – Prince Charming – and live, as they say, happily ever after.

When I was at the age of two, my parents started their second business, dealing in the importing and exporting of goods around the globe. Our business endeavors have allowed me to travel around the world, thereby facilitating my globetrotting adventures, many times over. I have met individuals from all walks of life, from many countries and regions, in every class.

I have met some of the most colorful and influential people – dignitaries – politicians – celebrities, et cetera. You can say that I have been blessed in life. Still, I did not meet Mr. Charming.

In each destination that I have traveled to, I have searched for him to no avail. Whether at Rio de Janeiro, Brazil; Capo San Lucas, Mexico; Athens, Greece; Penfield, Spain; Naples, Italy; the isolated villages of Brittany, France; Northern Ireland; Scotland's green valleys and rugged shores; the mountains of Kyrgyzstan; Belize; Honduras; The Maya in Guatemala; New York City; the outer banks of North Carolina or the California coast; no matter where I went and looked, the results were always the same. The Prince of my dreams had eluded me. That is, until fate – destiny – fortune – flexed their predetermined muscles.

I met my Prince in the most peculiar and unexpected way, and I did so in the United States. I was visiting with my aunt one day. It was an unplanned visit. Relevant to this time, I was having what you would call a recurring dream; so, given that my aunt has a gift of knowing how to interpret them, I decided to stop in to ask her about it. I was spending a month in America, with plans of returning back home to London.

Fate is one of those preordained forces that so intrigue our lives. While at my aunt's home, while she was on her phone, she had me wait in her sitting room. While I waited, I noticed a stack of documents on a table, and at the very top lay what I later learned was a manuscript (soon to be published) entitled: **"If I Had Only... Lived"**, written by a Celestino A. Colon. Clipped on its cover was a 4"x6" picture of the author. I was instantly drawn. Those Hazel eyes! I recall asking my aunt: "Who is This Man?" She went on to explain to me that he was a prisoner serving a life sentence in prison within the

Massachusetts (USA) Department of Correction. I distinctly recall telling myself: "What a pity – What a waste." At that moment, I recall feeling disappointed that he was not to be my Prince, yet his situation only served to pique my curiosity, and hello, those Hazel eyes! My aunt mentioned to me that she was planning on visiting with "Sal", as she referred to him, within that month. She asked for my opinion on his manuscript, if I were so inclined to read it, for what she said to be "input purposes." I, in all honesty, did so reluctantly. I was planning to take a breather, do a little R&R and enjoy the beach.

Reading Sal's manuscript has changed my life. Despite the fact that this man is in prison, serving a second degree life sentence, he has found a way to enrich my life. Sal's journey has been filled with much pain and suffering, but after being privileged to know all the pertinent parts of this man, I have come to believe that he will, given the opportunity, change the world and enrich people's lives, just as he has done so to mine. I have met and fallen deeply in love with my Prince – my fiancé – my future – my world. Finally, I have come to feel what all the great poets and writers down the ages rhapsodized about: True love – unconditional and pure love.

When I mentioned to Sal that I needed to write about him, knowing that is was very important to me, he simply made a gesture, conveying to me ever so reluctantly that it was okay (of course, he never denies me anything I ask). Sal's mission in life is to advocate, fight and litigate on behalf of prisoners, especially those he believes to be innocent. I have not met a man who is so dedicated, passionate and loyal. I know that he will feel awkward with this article, but I need to give a voice, so to speak, to what I know he won't do. He is a proud man, and yes, somewhat stubborn when he wants to be.

Not long ago, I was in a very serious car accident back home in London. I almost died. The accident left me with many, too many obstacles to endure – many surgeries. After I had waited a long time to meet my Prince, the answer to my most cherished dreams, and after falling in love with him, the thought that I might (I embraced myself) lose him broke my heart into smithereens. I had to reason with myself that this, my plight, would be too much of a burden on anyone to bear. I felt that no man, especially one that was half a world away and locked up in prison serving a life sentence, especially with everything that I knew about his treacherous past, well, it would all be too much to endure. Ultimately, believing that we would soon find ourselves to fend for ourselves in our own hells, I gave in to a deep depression. I was filled with an ineffable sense of loss. I remember feeling so lonely, afraid and desperate. I cried in my father's arms countless times. I felt as though my world was being taken away from me, one piece at a time. I had just finished saying goodbye to my own mother, not too long before that, which was close in time to Sal's brother Richard's death. I thought about Sal's life, how much of it had been enveloped in such misery. The loss of his beloved Michelle (his first love); his life in prison; the incidents that were inflicted upon him; the death of his father, his brother and so many of his close family and friends through the years. Oh, how I cried, believing that he would simply go back living his own solitary life. The pain and torment in this realization was overwhelming. I thought that I would die just from the emotional infliction alone. I was wrong. My prince spoke some magical words. These were the words that my prince conveyed to me in such a romantic manner: First, he (conspiring with both my sister Caitlen and my father) had me serenaded and presented me with beautiful romantic live music – roses – candlelight – chocolates – a charm – balloons – a giant Teddy Bear – flew in my extended family and close friends and proceeded to propose to me via proxy. Remember, I was in London, while he was in a prison in America! (We had no way of being physically together.)

What were the words that my Prince Charming so eloquently expressed in such a sentimental and poetic way? He said: "Babe, my love, when we first met, I was a broken man, a wretched soul, living in Hell on Earth, a prisoner serving a life sentence. We fell in love despite all that. Despite the odds. Despite our age difference (19 years). Despite all of me, you made me whole again. You had no reservations about my plight. Why? Why I ask? Why would I even contemplate continuing down this journey without my Princess? Remember, you saved my life. You gave it some meaning, purpose and joy. We are partners. Never forget our promises to each other 'what happens to you, happens to me'. You also know my motto: 'In life, don't ever shoot for the hills, shoot for the mountains, because the view is always better at the top'." He went on: "Even if I have to hold your hand, or need to carry you up that mountain, we will get there, together, I promise you." Then, with a voice disconcertingly devoid of emotion, he said: "My parents did not raise a coward. I have your back, no matter what." Then he reminded me of a promise he made my mother, right before she left this world. He wrote to her: "Your daughter had found it profoundly within her to entrust me to always treasure, protect and embrace her heart. She could go on to live 1,000 years, travel to every corner of the world, fly off to the galaxy, and she would not find a man to cherish that heart more. The day you depart from us, you can rest assured that your daughter's heart will never cry due to something that I've done. I promise."

Somehow, he found a goat and had my sister take a ring that was tied around its neck. She gave it to me, and he then asked me: "Are you willing to climb up that mountain with me. If you are, would you marry me?" That is my Prince Charming, my rock, my safe haven.

Later on, I was told that both my father and then my sister traveled to America to see him and to thank him for loving me unconditionally. My sister even asked me if there is a copy of him somewhere in this world. My dad loves him too (he finally has a son). My friends nicknamed him "Mr. Delicious." They all have met him. He has earned their love, respect and admiration. Our next step is to unite both our families, but first we need to have him paroled.

Prior to my mother departing, she once said this about Sal: "He is not a prisoner. There are no walls big enough or thick enough to keep him from the world." I now know what she meant. (See the next article, entitled **"A Call to Humanity"**. It was my mother's favorite.)

A Call to Humanity

For one to best understand the present plight facing prisoners within the United States, especially us, the "LIFERS", one must liken us to those who have previously fought the oppressive forces of inequality, fighting for Civil Rights, Civil Liberties and against all things that seem unjust. Here in America, there have been countless battles fought over the aforementioned. Whether it is related to "Afro-Americans" or "Women" or "Gays" or "Trans-genders", among other groups of underdogs fighting for equality and respect throughout American history, we can, without a doubt, add prisoners to that list as soldiers and allies in a war against those forces. I am extremely proud to be a soldier in this fight. I believe this fight to be a Human Rights issue. I believe that others have not canvassed this subject adequately enough. We prisoners have lived it. We have looked at it steadily, calmly, resolutely and at length defiantly, for a long time. Too long I suppose.

Protocol and common sense require that prisoners stand

back and let outside activists speak for us, defend us and lead us from behind the scene in our fight. This is the essence of prisoner politics. I do not necessarily believe this to be the correct approach. It is both good and reassuring to know that we have allies, but we must get up and fight our own battles. That is the way to win back our self-respect. That is the way to make these adversarial forces respect us. And if, for whatever reason, said forces will not let us live like men and women, they certainly cannot keep us from dying like one!

Now, let me be clear here. When I said "Fight", I am referring to **"Litigation"**, **"Education"**, **"Legislation"** and **"Adjudication"**. I am referring to fighting them in an articulate and intellectual manner, the pen being mightier than the sword. Whenever possible, we must ask the media for a platform to present a voice.

We should all be taking self-accountability of our very own actions. It is my wholehearted belief that every prisoner or subject of these tyrannical forces that does not challenge on the spot every instance of racism and/or discrimination committed against them, whether it be overt or covert, who choose to instead swallow their own spit and go on smiling, is a traitor to the fundamental principles which our founding fathers believed in. There may be those that would perceive them to be, just as I have, nothing more than pusillanimous individuals, without guts and who very well have to accept his or her own complicity in all of it. We need to approach this from a profound moral objective.

The question here is this: Are we going to listen to our conscience and silently remain in fear, or are we going to stand up and represent? We should represent everything that is good about the humane spirit: peace, harmony, love, fairness, respect, human sympathy, kindness and compassion for those around us. Let us be ambassadors of a non-violent world of peace.

Unfortunately, my past was not the most peaceful. I had come to believe myself to be a recalcitrant of all things unjust, fighting against those agents of oppression that seem to dehumanize us, the prisoners, especially those within the Massachusetts Department of Correction. I had a deep hatred towards all such authorities that oppress any human being due to financial reasons, who put financial gain above rehabilitation, such as those associated with the exploitation of prisoners.

Although the manner by which I approach these problems has changed (I come from a peaceful man's Christian perspective these days), I still feel passionately about such injustices.

We should be ashamed of the urbane and smiling hypocrisy we in general practice merely to exist in a world whose values we both envy and despise. Let us be honest here, we prisoners are treated no better than livestock, goods or any other merchandise available. In one word, we are "Prostitutes" for politicians. Some even say we are modern day "Slaves", only worth less than one-third of the free man. We are commodities for those same individuals that smile back at us on an everyday basis. These individuals go around professing, as they do here in Massachusetts, "we walk the toughest beat" within the criminal justice system, but we prisoners know the truth. Unfortunately, the mainstream media do not convey the truth.

We need to wake up as a society and get off our backs and support one another. Let us educate and inform one another, guiding the younger generation of men and women towards improving their lives in all facets, teaching them how to communicate with the courts and with our legislatures and how to litigate matters within our judicial system. Let us teach them to allocate their talents and assure them that with numbers comes power. Let us reach out to those in need of guidance and teach them to voice their opinions and grievances through editorials and any and all "Intellectual" weapons that can be utilized in fighting for what is essentially theirs. Let us show them the importance of informing the International community about our suffering and our plight. **Litigate – Educate – Legislate – Adjudicate.**

But, at the end of the day, we need to approach all of this with respect and honor and always with conviction from a loving and compassionate heart, not from a malicious one.

Furthermore, let us keep in mind that we are all bound to each other, not only by the ties of a common humanity, but by the more tender relations as parents, wives, husbands, children, brothers, sisters, friends and, above all, as members of something much more important than ourselves. Our condition, our plight, our situation, does not absolve us from our moral obligations. Let us change one heart at a time – one life at a time – one community, and then, and only then…

Have you not seen enough? All I have seen around me within these prison walls is humanity supplicating with tears and wisdom urging her solemn plea. The current prison "industries" are one of the peculiarities of all American institutions. Just look around yourselves. Look closely. There is political "Oppression", economic "Exploitation" and social "Degradation." We prisoners have been treated with sovereign indifference, coldness and scorn. We in general make voluntary submission each and every day. **Enough!!!**

Let us make choices that build up individuals and not tear them down. Let us spread the word that if we all did our part, sooner or later the antithesis of justice will lose its claim on us. Let us be led by a loving and conscious heart – a spirit that does not allow malicious and hurtful acts to dictate our actions.

It breaks my heart to see that while our country advances in civilization, prosperity and happiness, cultivating things which appertain to literature, science and law, our correctional system is breeding a new age system of "slaves." There is a deeply cruel prejudice and profound hatred in the bosom of the correctional system in this country. It breeds hatred and a "pay back" attitude in the lives of prisoners and their families. It is unavoidable. The current correctional institutions in the United States have done this to make us subservient to their own purpose – their financial gains. Here in Massachusetts they seem to perfect this.

If we are going to be honest here, let us call things the way we see them. Prisoners in this country, especially from my point of view in Massachusetts, are treated as nothing more than commodities. They have transgressed constitutional and natural limits. Any person that keeps things in an unbiased perspective can see that the plight of prisoners is an effort to nationalize, perpetuate and extend "slavery", but by another name, "incarceration." Society seems to be oblivious to the fact that this evil of gross and monstrous abominations, this evil of the great organic crop that these institutions are breeding, creates a negative ripple effect on society for future generations to have to deal with. But truth has its way of finding the cracks and the openings in whatever walls of make-believe they set up.

People all over the United States need to be woken. We should be doing positive and constructive things to counter all the negative and evil acts employed concerning the manner by which we treat not only our prisoners but anyone that is under our authority. We have to treat others in a humane way. Let us send an earthquake of a voice throughout this land. We need to double our efforts. At a time like this, when politics seems to dictate every aspect of our lives, scorching irony, not convincing argument, is in need. Imagine: the so-called "Correctional" arm of law enforcement is breeding more criminals or, at least, poking the bear as they say – Foxes guarding the hen-house.

If you doubt what I am trying to say, simply ask yourselves two simple yet important questions: 1) Why would many correctional departments around this country find the need to employ the services of a public relations personnel/company? 2) When was the last time you read about or heard of a former prisoner going out into society and contributing something positive? Well, they are out there. But no, not one positive story, just simple good ol' fashioned propaganda.

Had I the ability to reach the masses, I would pour out a teary stream of bitching ridicule, withering sarcasm, blasting reproach and a stern rebuke at the hypocrisy I see all around me. Do I dare to name them? Let me see?...

We live in a nation that conveys to the world the importance of a "Free Nation" – "Democracy" and "Human Rights" and "Civil Rights." Yet, we the prisoners of this country have been harshly treated. Our collective intellect has been destroyed. They have attempted to shut out from our minds every ray of light. Our voices and our votes have been taken away. We are constantly being used in a specific manner for gerrymandering purposes. Our shouts for equality, liberty and justice hollow mockery, even long after we have paid our debts to society. We are constantly met with Civil and Human Rights filibustering by our very own Legislative branch (as a whole), while our Judicial branch is conspiring with them as our beloved Executive branch deals with us in the most condescending manner. And let us not forget that in addition to the aforementioned, the so-called "Correctional" arm of our Criminal Justice system plays a game with everyone, especially the public, every time they feed them with misinformation, misleading them at every turn.

Our Criminal Justice system plays a role as well. It endeavors to make us as much brutes as possible, for their financial gain. They have conditioned us to be fully dependent on them as much as possible. They have slowly been taking away all tools that prisoners would need to better themselves, such as education and avocations. Thus, they create job security for themselves by securing a revolving door system instead of creating positive changes in human lives. They do not allow us a chance to contribute into something, anything positive, so that we could become productive members of society.

This is why I dare to call into question and to denounce with all the emphasis I can command everything that seems to perpetuate oppression. I will not equivocate; I will not excuse ignorance, and I sure will not be silent. The conscience of America, of all citizens, should be woken. Our nation must be roused. I desire to remove the misunderstanding that has been created in the minds of millions of Americans in their perception of us prisoners. Despite the impression given by all the propaganda, many of us prisoners do care about the future of this great country of ours. And if our legislature, especially those that put up a good "front", will do nothing but spend their time wasted on non-essential things and matters of non-importance, then let us inform our international communities. Let us convey to them the fact that Human Rights are being violated right here in America, in Massachusetts. Let us rise up and pick up our intellectual weapons of choice: Litigate, Educate, Legislate and Advocate.

FINALLY, GINA

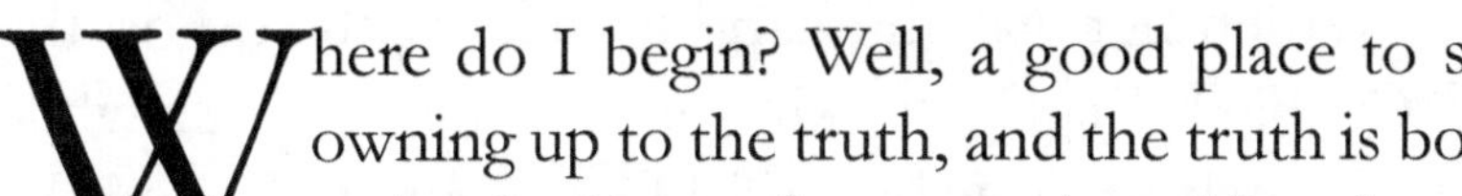

Where do I begin? Well, a good place to start is by owning up to the truth, and the truth is both simple and sobering at the same time. Here is one simple and sobering fact: Of all the individuals I can list that I both hurt the most in life and that I regret profoundly doing so, I would have to list you first – right on top of that list.

There are no words to describe the feeling of regret and guilt I carry daily within myself. Regret for not allowing you to break down the walls that I built around my shattered heart at the time that we were together, and guilt for breaking your precious heart. You were nothing but good to me. If the truth be told, you were also good for me. Yet, driven by the pain I endured, an immense heartache, and the distrust I felt towards the world in general, I somehow lost myself. I was drowning in self-pity, and I took you down with me.

I failed to see the beauty in life. The simple things, if I had allowed them to penetrate my heart, would have served to enrich my life. Simply put, I failed to appreciate you for what you were and what you represented, and that was a lifeline that I refused to hold onto due to the state of mind I was in.

I am so sorry. I have managed to exist these past three decades in an environment devoid of hope and dreams. Considering the callous manner that I lived my life when I was younger, especially during the time relevant to us, a time when we were supposed to be building a future together, I failed you, pure and simple. You gave 100% of yourself while I contributed, at best, 10%. I guess prison was a good place for me after all. I never got over, at least during those days, the profound hurt that was inflicted upon me, and you were there, unfortunately, as collateral damage.

You came so close to mending my heart, if only I had allowed it. I remember walking hand in hand with you on the shores of Orchard Beach, looking into your eyes, all while taking in every inch of your beautiful face, your smile, and the smell of your perfume. I contemplated tearing down the walls around my heart, but I did not allow myself such freedom. I have come to regret this more than anything else in this world. Whenever I look back on my life (which is full of regrets and What Ifs?), you have come to represent my number one What If? What if I allowed myself to feel loved?

I pray to God that over these past years you have lived a life which is both full and rewarding. I hope that every day you have a reason to smile and enjoy those little moments with family and friends. Whenever I think about you, I remember your smile, your laugh and the sparkle in your eyes.

It is my sincere hope that my actions did not rob the world of the beauty you had to give. By this, I mean that I hope and pray I did not change you in a negative manner. With time, and with God's grace, I have come to learn to appreciate you.

The Lord has blessed me in so many ways. I cannot begin to describe the profound love I feel for those, like you, that have enriched my life, even though at the time I did not know it. I have a very special prayer that I pray, especially for you and your family. May God bless you and keep you and your family safe. **Again, I am sorry.**

A Mother's Love

Despite the fact that I have spent many years of my incarcerated life fighting for justice, peace and freedom, I can honestly say I feel blessed. You see, despite my plight, I can look back on my life knowing that I have been blessed, profoundly so.

I think about those that have played a major positive role in my life and the ways that they have enriched my life, and I say to myself: The Lord has blessed me! I think about my late father and it warms my heart knowing that he loved me. I think about my siblings: My late brother Richard and, as I cite within Chapter 8 of this book, "Everything that he did was to put family first." My sister Joann, who has been there for me throughout this ordeal, every step of the way. And my little sister Arlene and her beautiful disposition. You have to meet her to appreciate her. Then we have Paige. She came into my life at its darkest, only to shine a light on me. There have been many others, such as my Aunt Hilda, who I refer to as my second mom. There are my cousins: Janet, Jessica and Yvonne who convey to me that they love me and are there for me. Then there is my cousin Ray who I have always thought of as another brother to me. Even my brother-in-law Edwin has brought me some warm memories and joy. Yes, I am blessed.

The Lord has indeed brought joy and love into my life despite my actions, despite the environment that I live in. But, there is yet a whole new level when I think about the profound love and joy I feel whenever my mother Edna comes to mind.

My mother Edna has sacrificed so much, all in order to ensure that her children had and continue to have a fighting chance of becoming good and moral individuals. She, coupled with my dad, not only did her best in protecting us (my siblings and me) but also made sure that through words and deeds she conveyed to us that we were and continue to be loved. I seem to not be able to put into words the love that I feel whenever I look back on my life, especially when I think about moments that I had spent with my mother. Though I was one of four, the second oldest, she somehow found a way to make each and every one of her children feel as though we were her favorite. She conveyed to us, simply in the manner that she loves her children, that this world needs each and every one of us, and that we are special. That we, if given the opportunity, could make this world a better place than when we came into it.

My mother has always been a nurturer and epitomizes the role of a true loving mother. She was a fun mother while raising her children, yet she was strict when she needed to be. She would take time for each of us. I love my mother to the point of not being able to convey such love into words. There are no words that can convey how I feel.

There is a reason why, any time there are family gatherings, members of our family light up whenever they first see her. I am so proud of her.

REFLECTION OF OUR FAILURES

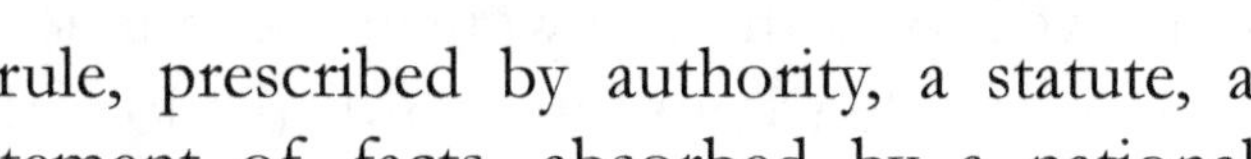

There is a rule, prescribed by authority, a statute, a formal statement of facts, absorbed by a national phenomenon. In plain English: the Law.

When someone is accused of breaking the law, we settle this dispute within our judicial system. As we should all know, our judicial system is the administration of justice. It is where all our legal discrepancies are sorted. It is made up of different departments, with one destination. Its invisible necessity is to sort out and carry out all rules and laws that are prescribed by authority.

Ask yourself these three questions: 1) How many of us Americans truly believe in our judicial system? 2) Are all Americans treated equally within our judicial system? And 3) How about "Justice"? – Can and do we Americans find justice within our judicial system?

Given my own personal experiences and experiences in assisting others, I would have to answer a resounding NO!!! to all three aforementioned questions. I do not believe in our judicial system. I do not believe that all Americans are treated equally within our judicial system, and I strongly believe that our judicial system is not administrating the kind of justice that was intended by our founding fathers.

When you take into account the thousands of cases that I have worked on through the years, it comes across as somewhat oxymoronic to make the statement that I do not believe in said system while I file thousands of documents in an attempt to litigate and/or adjudicate matters in my attempt of finding the resolution to problems. If the truth be told, in a selective few cases, I find that the system does work to some degree. It is that my cynicism through the years has taken its toll on my outlook in such a system where I have experienced that the playing field is not level, especially the poorer and/or the less educated a person is.

We need to change this broken system. There are things that we can incorporate, where we can find justice, all while issuing just and fair punishments for crime. We owe it to society to have a system in place that is fair, just and allows for atonement in a manner where lives are changed in a positive way. Presently, there is no system in place that affords mechanisms to play a role in a person's life where they are given incentives of wanting and seeing that they need to change their lives and turn their lives around. Changing the trajectory of their destination can play a positive role in someone's life, where in turn it can create positive ripple effects throughout all facets of society. I have seen too many issues relative to the indigent individuals and the manner they are treated, which is different to those that have the financial means to pay for, let's say, a defense in a criminal case.

Take the issue of "Rehabilitation". We as a society seem

to have the wrong approach in dealing with this issue. We in general have the "lock them up and throw away the key" mentality, or we constantly use monetary reasons why we can not effectively rehabilitate people. I strongly disagree with either one of these approaches.

Let us address this issue from a common sense perspective: **Specific Deterrence**, that is, deterrence of a particular defendant from committing further crime, has as its basic inherent flaw the inability to be flexible, although it may certainly be individualized.

For example, a particular defendant may be specifically deterrable, and if this is the case, his arrest, trial and conviction will have already deterred him from any future participation in criminal activity and no sentence is necessary.

On the other hand, if he is not deterrable, then no sentence will be effective as a psychological motivation, although incarceration would certainly be a specific deterrent. However, in that case, the only useful sentence is one of total and eternal incarceration, which, in addition to posing certain constitutional problems based upon cruel and unusual punishment grounds, would also defeat the purpose of other valuable sentencing objectives.

Specific deterrence, then, in terms of sentencing by way of incarceration, must always be tempered with respect to the goals of sentencing due to the fact that it possesses the potential to be counterproductive.

General deterrence is the sentencing concept probably considered most important from the government's point of view, although it is unlikely that a particular defendant will be very interested in whether or not his sentence has a deterrent effect on anyone else.

Since the government's primary objective is the protection of the public interest, general deterrence is certainly a viable sentencing objective, although it is difficult to determine the possibility of its success on such a large universe as the general public. It is more likely, therefore, that the government's objective regarding the concept of general deterrence in a particular case is simply to see to it that the small universe of potential transgressors understand that if any of them are convicted of a similar crime, s/he will be subjected to penalties.

Rehabilitation, of course, is the objective most important to a defendant in sentencing and that includes, to a certain extent, specific deterrence, and to a lesser degree, general deterrence. It is also the objective least capable of definition but most capable of accomplishment, when it is approached with the proper prospective. With regard to rehabilitation, there are individuals that are prime candidates to use this theory, but the Massachusetts Department of Correction (DOC) looks to others that are not worthy candidates.

You may wonder why the Massachusetts Department of Correction chooses many prisoners that are not worthy for, let's say, parole, lower security, et cetera, over those that are actually better candidates. It is my strong opinion that they do this because these individuals are used as some kind of pawn in this game called 'revolving door', thus allowing this business to continue to thrive.

It is the department's obligation, in attempting to attain the objective of rehabilitation, to first define it. The concept of rehabilitation itself presupposes the state of **"habilitation"** at some prior time. In each case viewed, the DOC should look into each (a) family background; (b) employment history; (c) educational background; (d) professional accomplishment;

and (e) character development. Instead, the DOC uses some method other than common sense.

It should be noted that what is specifically applicable herein is both rehabilitation, by its standard mode of concentration on the development of alternatives to criminal behavior, and its potential disadvantages. It is at this point that the theory of incarceration interacts to produce a workable solution to the sentencing problem.

The department's tasks, therefore, become the application of the most expeditious means of achieving the two most important sentencing objectives available: general deterrence and rehabilitation as modified by the theory of specific deterrence. All this seems to go without practice within the Massachusetts Department of Correction.

In all my years of incarceration, I have not been able to understand their angle. I have seen too many men leave prison with no money, education or direction. All their years incarcerated were wasted. Not from their own making, but due to the department's actions, or lack of actions. They seem to concentrate on taking away all tools a person needs to better be equipped to succeed once released from prison.

I have concluded one thing about the Massachusetts Department of Correction, and that is if any businesses here in American ran their everyday business like this department, well, they would go bankrupt.

'Maybe When I'm Gone'

Do you ever take time to think about me? –
About the simple times we've spent together?
If you close your eyes, do you see me?
Or whenever I'm not around, Do you miss me?
'Maybe When I'm Gone' 'Maybe When I'm Gone'
What would I give, so that you would forgive me?
Would you be there standing waiting for me with open
arms? –
Waiting to accept the profound love that I feel for you?
Would you smile or cry when we hold on to each other?
'Maybe When I'm Gone' 'Maybe When I'm Gone'
Would you shed one tear for me? –
If I were to leave this world –
Would your heart break? Would your heart yearn for me?
Would you lose one night of sleep, thinking of me?
'Maybe When I'm Gone' 'Maybe When I'm Gone'
Do you know that I would give my life for you?
What would you do if you knew today would be my last?

Would you hold me – love me – touch me?
Would you let me in your world? – If only just for one night?
'Maybe When I'm Gone' 'Maybe When I'm Gone'
Do you know that I've given my life to our Lord? –
And I pray for Him to bless you?
Do you know that I've searched all my life for peace? –
Only to find it in a place that surprised me to see? – PRISON
'Maybe When I'm Gone' 'Maybe When I'm Gone'
Written on August 05, 2013
Dedicated to past relationships

A Small Church with a Bright Light

The Greek word '**ekklesia**' refers to any assembly and applies to local bodies of believers or to the universal body of all believers. '**Ekklesia**' is the Greek word for church.

The Church's identity as the people of God is seen throughout the Bible in terms of both Jewish and Gentile ("Pagan") people alike.

The Church is not merely a sectarian religious society. In fact, the Bible tell us that Jesus, the central figure and the fundamental person of the Christian faith, speaks of personally building this new community on the confession of His Lordship (see Matthew 16: 18-19).

Within Old Colony Correctional Center in Bridgewater, a prison within the Massachusetts Department of Correction, there is a small unit where you will find members of a small church, most of whom are LIFERS. These men come from all walks of life. There are Catholics and Protestants working together, putting aside all differences with the goal of doing God's will.

These men are of strong faith. They are good Christian men, and they live up to the principles of Christianity. They try to be each other's checks and balances without being over-bearing. They are not perfect, but they try to do what is correct. I am proud to say that I belong to this church. The Greek suffix '**-ianos**' was originally applied to slaves. Members of this small church do understand that a Christian is a slave or adherent of Christ – one committed to Christ; a follower of Christ. We try to live up to our obligation as members of God's Church.

We, despite our size, take our responsibility very seriously. We are constantly reminded of the two greatest commandments given to us by Jesus Christ Himself: "Love the Lord your God with all your heart and with all your soul and with all your mind," and "Love your neighbor as yourself." (Matthew 22:37-39)

In addition to the members of our church, we have a group of volunteers that come in despite our plight and our reputation. They visit us despite who we are. They do not judge us or look down at us. Nor do they convey to us that they are better than we are. On the contrary, these individuals treat each and every one of us as what we are: "Brothers-in-Christ". They have accepted us into the family of believers and we are made stronger in faith because of it.

These volunteers: Kevin and Jen, Walter and Martha, Kevin and Betsy, Chuck, Tom, Rick and Bob, come into this prison and allow God to use them to accomplish His work. They are led by the spirit of volunteerism, prompted by devotion to God.

The Bible speaks of the spirit of volunteerism throughout. It has allowed magnificent acts to occur with God's blessing and direction. It has enabled daunting tasks to be accomplished. Take Moses for example. He received voluntary contributions of precious goods from the Israelites sufficient to construct the tabernacle (see Exodus 25:1-9). And even a widow without means gave willingly (see Luke 21:1-4). In financial giving, the lead in volunteerism was normally taken by persons who had the means to give. As I mentioned, these were people who were led by God Himself to accomplish His work. Others have contributed their time and skills. These types of individuals give of themselves without expecting anything in return other than knowing they are doing God's will.

So yes, these volunteers give of themselves in a Christlike manner. Every Monday night (with the exception of during the COVID-19 Pandemic Quarantine), Kevin and his wife Jen, Walter and his wife Martha, Kevin and his wife Betsy, and Chuck, come into Old Colony Correctional Center – a place that, if the truth be told, without God's grace would be dismal – and they display the type of love and caring which the Bible directs each believer to have. The same can be said of Tom, who comes in every Friday night for studies and fellowship, and Rick and Bob, who come in on Saturday afternoons.

In addition, we have our Catholic volunteers and support group: Father Frank, Father Bill and Father Jason, as well as two laymen, Paul and Jay, who meet with us on Sunday mornings and/or Sunday evenings.

These aforementioned volunteers, in addition to having the spirit of volunteerism, have the Fruit of the Spirit: "love, joy, peace, forbearance, kindness, goodness, faithfulness, gentleness and self-control." (Galatians 5:22-23)

We are a blessed church. We have the tools a good church needs to lead its members to do God's will. We have, in addition to the selfless volunteers, not one but two men to lead us. These good shepherds, Deacon A.J. Constantino and Pastor Nathan Hays, lead by example. They teach us and demonstrate to us the importance of putting our differences aside and working together in the name of love and, much more importantly, in the name of Jesus Christ.

Whenever I think about all these individuals, I cannot help but feel their love for us. The Bible tells us that it is important to love others.

In fact, 1 Corinthians 13:13 conveys to us that we are given eternal gifts in life: "Faith, hope and love. But the greatest of these is love." The Bible also conveys to us that "Love is patient, love is kind. It does not envy, it does not boast, it is not proud. It does not dishonor others, it is not self-seeking, it is not easily angered, it keeps no record of wrongs. Love does not delight in evil but rejoices with the truth. It always protects, always trusts, always hopes, always perseveres. Love never fails." (1 Corinthians 13:4-8a)

The men in our church, along with the volunteers and our two shepherds, have demonstrated to me the importance of putting others' needs ahead of ourselves (see Philippians 2:3-4).

Our church, as the title of this piece suggests, is "A Small Church with a Bright Light." This is possible because the group of Christian men (most of whom are serving a life sentence) search out one another to break bread, pray, study, laugh, love, et cetera, all by keeping God as the center of our lives. I see our church as something special.

Each and every day, I see men around me taking their

responsibilities very seriously. On any given day, I witness Luis "Pucho" Lopez going around cleaning up after everyone, not because he has to but because he has taken, with God's grace, the responsibility to make sure that our place of worship is always in order and ready for us whenever we need to pray and worship. He has demonstrated to me the importance of service to others. Taking Jesus as our ultimate example, the New Testament pictures our Lord Jesus as the Suffering Servant fulfilling the glorious description in chapter fifty-three of Isaiah. In refusing to let his disciples reveal his true identity, Jesus was the Suffering Servant who did not strive or cry out (see Matthew 12:14-21). Therefore, in the resurrection and ascension, God glorified Jesus the Servant (see Acts 3:13). Pucho serves others with a smile and a twinkle in his eyes.

I also see it in others in our small church. I see it in Lewis "Luie" Lent as he makes himself available for anyone that may need his assistance in writing a letter or some institutional business. I see it in Jacques "J.R." Robidoux as he leads us in Bible studies every Monday, Tuesday, Friday and Sunday morning, teaching lessons that prepare and equip us for the day ahead. He personally prepares and studies for each lesson he teaches, and he does so with a genuine and loving heart. I see it in Neil Entwistle as he takes his time to tutor others in preparation for their HiSET exams, in addition to teaching us Biblical Greek and Hebrew, among other subjects.

I see the selfless acts of my Christian brothers all around me. Such actions have demonstrated to me the outworking of the Christian life and have ultimately influenced me in wanting to do God's will and to be of service to others. It is contagious.

Then I think of others within our church who, with the Grace of God, go around doing things that one can easily miss. But, if you pay attention, you will recognize these men as doing their part, all for the glory of God. Take Christopher Reardon who, along with J.R., brings joy to our services with musical instruments. Christopher also takes it upon himself to furnish us with reading materials every month. Then there is Paul Leahy who, along with Romano Ferraro, blesses us with art work, which we then send to our families.

I cannot help but feel the love within all facets of our church. We are Brothers-in-Christ that seem to know and embrace our roles – our parts within the church. Whether it is Irwin "Bud" Hartford, who serves as our "Altar boy" and also furnishes cool drinks to volunteers on hot days, or Stanley "Skippy" Benoit, who is our Scripture reader during Monday-night Bible studies. We have become accustomed to Ramon Fontanez's jokes (our church's de facto comedian), keeping us nice and loose. We are a church, a good small church, a close unit.

In addition, our church is blessed with having not one but two of what I like to refer to as "Walking Encyclopedias" in Gary Mercure and Romano Ferraro. We have intellectuals among us. And, let me not be remiss in mentioning Pedro Martinez, who constantly gives of himself, without reserve or in expectation of receiving glory. What a gentleman.

One thing I can say about our church is that we rally around a problem simply by bringing any problems that we may have to the Lord in prayer. When a prisoner within our unit has a medical emergency, we drop what we are doing to pray for him, in a small recreation yard of all places. We came together when another prisoner passed away (Michael Donovan, who was very popular and well liked), supporting those that were closest to him such as J.R., his cellmate for well past a decade.

We also have non-Christians that we as a unit support and

embrace. For example, Rabbi Chaim Zirkind is a very well liked person. He meets with us every Sunday, offering us lessons and insight on Jewish history, culture and faith. We have learned much from him and our lives are richer because of him.

In conclusion, I say this: It has been said that love is the unselfish, loyal and benevolent intention and commitment toward another. If this is true, I can say without any reservations: Our church is full of love.

Biblical love has God as its object. Love is a fruit of the Holy Spirit.

Yes, our church is small. but it certainly shines brightly. Our newest member, Keith Cox, is another great brother in God's family. May our Lord guide and protect him.

This chapter is dedicated to all volunteers that walk into prisons all around the world and meet with men and women that are looked upon as the least of the least. May God bless each and every one of you.

Celestino "Sal" Colon

ACKNOWLEDGMENTS

First and foremost, I need to give thanks to God for allowing me to find the small blessings in life throughout the day. And for giving me the strength to attack whatever trials and tribulations are thrown my way with grace.

To my family: My mother **Edna** for being the most supportive and greatest cheerleader of her children. My two sisters, **Joann** and **Arlene**, for being the best sisters any brother could hope for. My aunt **Hilda Santiago**, my second mother for being such an angel to those around her. To my cousins **Janet Morales, Jessica Santiago,** and **Yvonne Cunningham**, for their love and support. To my cousin **Ray Suarez** (my second brother) enough said. And my brother-in-law **Edwin Rivera**.

Also to all my boys: Jacques Robidoux, Neil Entwistle, Christopher Reardon, Ramon Fontanez, Romano Ferraro, Ariel Hernandez, Edwin Alemany, Pedro Martinez, Luis "Pucho" Lopez, Stanley Benoit, Paul Leahy, Lewis Lent, Irwin Hartford, Gary Mercure, Leo Womack, Thomas "Tommy" Hutchinson, Richard Hutchinson, Isaias "Mexico" Rodriguez, Mike Foster, Greg Martino, Anthony "Ant" Colaboro, Robert Shelly, Gordon Haas, Timothy Muise, Luis Perez, Arthur "AJ" Crawford, Kyle Fuchs, Shawn Michaels, Paul Maher, Ramon "Pitchy" Cruz, Kurt Kegler, Hector Blanco, Brian Peixoto, Thomas Crouse, John Keegan, Peter Contos, Emilio Castro, Patrick O'Shea, Dirk Greinder, Kirk Furnette, Vinny Nunez, Daniel Holland, Ronald Ward, Kenny Perry, Edgar Sanchez and a very special thank you to my girl Teresa Brugleria, You are my inspiration.

Prison Volunteers:

<u>Monday Night Group:</u> Kevin & Jen, Walter & Martha,

Kevin & Betsy, Chuck

<u>Friday Night:</u> Tom

<u>Saturday Afternoon:</u> Rick & Bob

<u>Book Club:</u> Bruce & Lynn

I would be remiss not to mention:

Leslie Walker, Lauren Petit, Kurt "The Librarian" Eichner, and Carolyn Murphy (NCCI Librarian), Deacon A.J. Constantino, Pastor Nathan Hays and Rabbi Chaim Zirkind, Father Frank, Father Bill, Father Jason, and Catholic Volunteers Paul and Jay.

ABOUT THE AUTHOR

Celestino "Sal" Colon is a prisoner serving a second-degree life sentence in Massachusetts. Though eligible for parole since 2010, he refuses to meet with the Parole Board for personal reasons.

He has spent the past three decades fighting for prisoner rights and prison reform.

He has served on the Board of Directors of Prison Legal Services (formerly Massachusetts Correctional Legal Services) since 2001.

He is presently working on two other books and can be reached at:

Celestino Colon (W-61629)
Old Colony Correctional Center
One Administration Road
Bridgewater, Massachusetts 02324
Or via E-Mail at:
CorrLinks.com

www.ingramcontent.com/pod-product-compliance
Lightning Source LLC
Chambersburg PA
CBHW071453030726
47593CB00003B/984